A Day in the Life: Rainforest Animals

# Poison Dart Frog

Anita Ganeri

**www.raintreepublishers.co.uk**
Visit our website to find out more information about Raintree books.

**To order:**
☎ Phone 0845 6044371
🖷 Fax +44 (0) 1865 312263
🖳 Email myorders@raintreepublishers.co.uk

Customers from outside the UK please telephone +44 1865 312262

Raintree is an imprint of Capstone Global Library Limited, a company incorporated in England and Wales having its registered office at 7 Pilgrim Street, London, EC4V 6LB – Registered company number: 6695582

Edited by Nancy Dickmann, Rebecca Rissman, and Catherine Veitch
Designed by Steve Mead
Picture research by Mica Brancic
Originated by Capstone Global Library
Printed and bound in China by South China Printing Company Ltd

ISBN 978 1 4062 1787 2 (hardback)
14 13 12 11 10
10 9 8 7 6 5 4 3 2 1

**British Library Cataloguing in Publication Data**
Ganeri, Anita
Poison dart frog. -- (A day in the life. Rainforest animals)
597.8'77-dc22
A full catalogue record for this book is available from the British Library.

**Acknowledgements**
We would like to thank the following for permission to reproduce photographs: Corbis **pp. 15, 18**(© Michael & Patricia Fogden), **22** (© Paul Souders); FLPA **pp. 9, 10, 19, 23 tadpole** (Minden Pictures/Thomas Marent), **14, 17, 20, 23 blow dart** (Minden Pictures/Mark Moffett), **16** (Minden Pictures/Albert Lleal); Nature Picture Library **p. 13** (© Tim Laman); Photolibrary **pp. 4** (age fotostock/Peter Lilja), **6, 23 poisonous** (age fotostock/Andoni Canela), **7** (Fotosearch), **11** (Oxford Scientific (OSF)/Brian Kenney), **12, 23 prey** (Mauritius/Rauschenbach Rauschenbach), **21** (Design Pics Inc/Corey Hochachka); Shutterstock **pp. 5, 23 amphibian** (Pavel Mikoska), **23 rainforest** (© Szefei).

Cover photograph of poison dart frog on moss reproduced with permission of Corbis (© Joe McDonald).

Back cover photographs of (left) a poison dart frog's tongue reproduced with permission of Photolibrary (Mauritius/ Rauschenbach Rauschenbach); and (right) a poison dart tadpole reproduced with permission of Corbis (© Michael & Patricia Fogden).

We would like to thank Michael Bright for his invaluable help in the preparation of this book.

# Contents

Some words are in bold, **like this**. You can find them in the glossary on page 23.

# What are poison dart frogs?

Poison dart frogs are tiny frogs.

There are many different types of poison dart frog.

toad

Poison dart frogs belong to a group of animals called **amphibians**.

Toads, newts, and salamanders are also amphibians.

# What do poison dart frogs look like?

Poison dart frogs can be yellow, blue, green, red, black, or orange.

Their brightly coloured skin is **poisonous**.

The bright colours make the frogs easy for birds and other animals to see.

The colours warn these animals that the frogs are not good to eat.

# Where do poison dart frogs live?

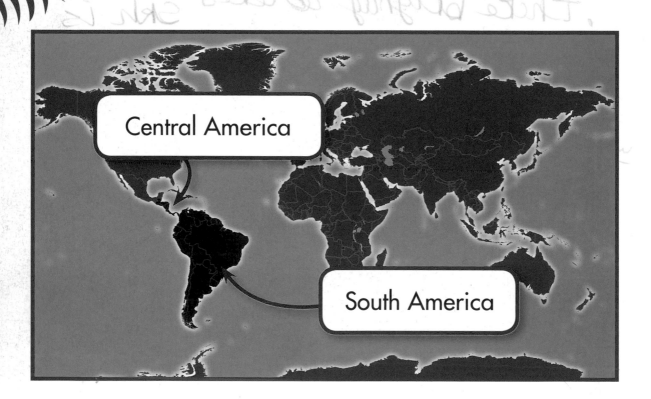

Poison dart frogs live in the **rainforests** of Central and South America.

It is warm and wet in the rainforest all the year round.

Most poison dart frogs live on the forest floor.

They shelter under rocks and plants, close to small streams or pools.

# What do the frogs do in the day?

Poison dart frogs are very active in the day.

They search for food on the forest floor and look after their young.

Some poison dart frogs live in small groups.

Others live in pairs of one male and one female.

# What do poison dart frogs eat?

tongue

Poison dart frogs eat tiny insects and spiders.

They grab their **prey** with long, sticky tongues and pull it into their mouths.

insect

The frogs get their poison from the insects they eat.

In turn, the insects get their poison from the plants that they feed on.

# Does anything hunt poison dart frogs?

blow dart

Some **rainforest** people catch poison dart frogs.

They put the frogs' poison on **blow darts** to kill animals for food.

poison dart frog

Most rainforest animals leave poison dart frogs alone.

But the fire-bellied snake likes eating the frogs and is not hurt by their poison.

# Where are the baby frogs born?

eggs

Some poison dart frogs lay their eggs on the forest floor.

Other poison dart frogs lay their eggs on leaves.

eggs

The eggs are covered in jelly to stop them drying out.

The parents guard the eggs for about two weeks until they hatch into tiny **tadpoles**.

# Do poison dart frogs look after their young?

tadpole

Poison dart frogs are caring parents.

When the **tadpoles** hatch, the parents carry them to water where they can grow into frogs.

The water may be a small pond, or a pool of rainwater inside a leaf.

The parents feed the tadpoles on plants, young insects, and eggs that did not hatch.

# What do the frogs do at night?

At night, poison dart frogs do not go to sleep in the same way that you do.

Instead, they sit very still and rest.

Some poison dart frogs like to rest under piles of leaves on the forest floor.

Other frogs rest in small holes in the ground.

# Poison dart frog body map

body

skin

eye

leg

mouth

toe

# Glossary

**amphibian** animal that lives partly on water and partly on land

**blow dart** pointed dart used for hunting

**poisonous** may cause illness or death

**prey** animal that is hunted by other animals for food

**rainforest** thick forest with very tall trees and a lot of rain

**tadpole** young frog

## Books

*Rainforest Animals (Focus on Habitats)*, Stephen Savage (Wayland, 2006)
*Usborne Beginners: Rainforest*, Lucy Beckett-Bowman (Usborne, 2008)

## Websites

www.itsnature.org/ground/amphibians-land/poison-dart-frog/
http://kids.nationalgeographic.com/Animals/CreatureFeature/
Poison-dart-frog

# Index